This book
belongs to:

LET'S
TALK

When my parents forgot how to be friends

Written by Jennifer Moore-Mallinos

Illustrated by Marta Fàbrega

SALARIYA
BH
BOOK HOUSE

4

My parents used to be friends. We did everything together. Every Saturday we had a special family night. We were always laughing, and had so much fun. Sometimes we played board games, and other times we watched a movie and ate popcorn. No matter what we did, we were always together.

I knew my parents were forgetting how to be friends because things started to change. Sometimes I would wake up late at night and hear my parents arguing. I didn't know what they were arguing about, but they seemed very angry, and my Mum usually cried.

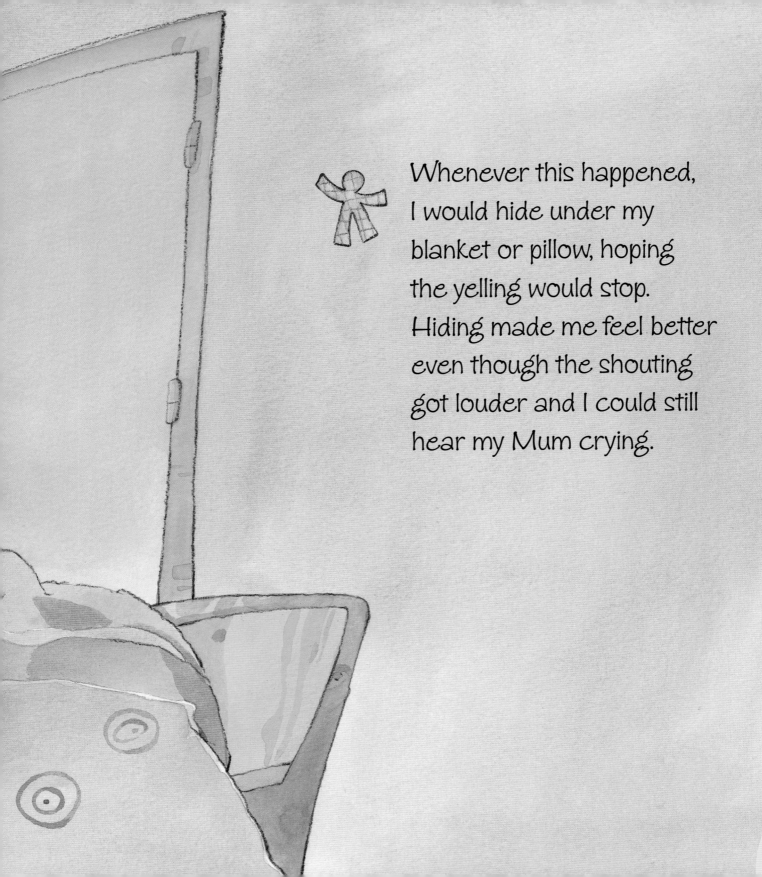

Whenever this happened, I would hide under my blanket or pillow, hoping the yelling would stop. Hiding made me feel better even though the shouting got louder and I could still hear my Mum crying.

I knew my parents were forgetting to be friends because they often looked so sad. They didn't talk to one another very much, and we even stopped having family night. I couldn't even remember the last time we laughed together.

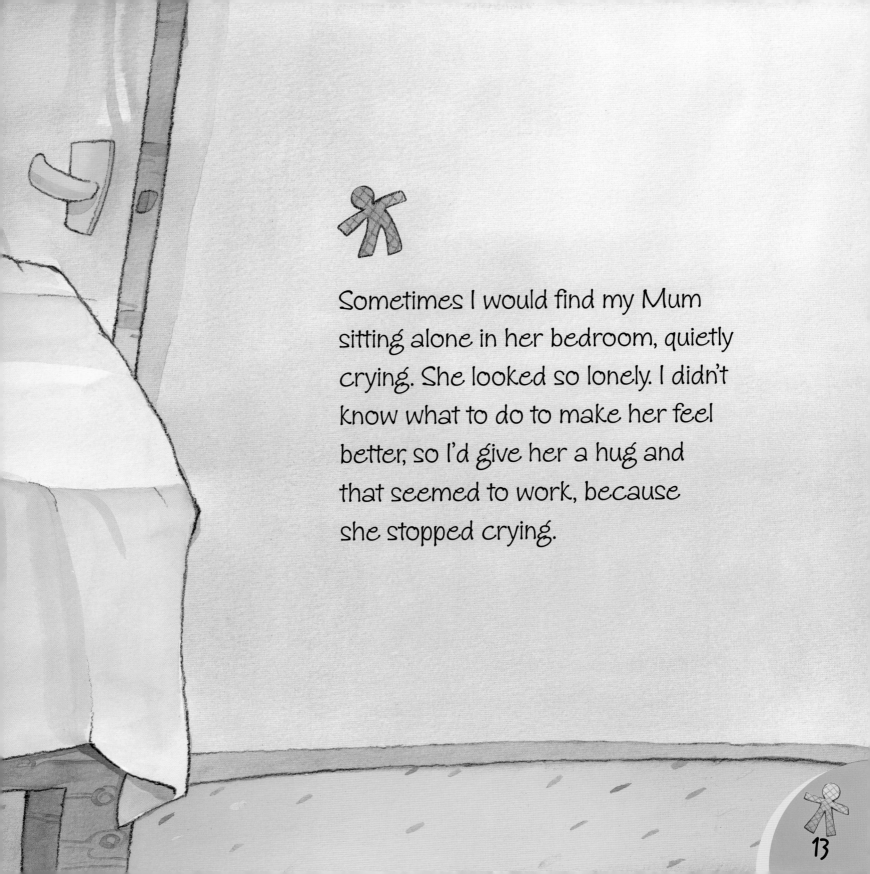

Sometimes I would find my Mum sitting alone in her bedroom, quietly crying. She looked so lonely. I didn't know what to do to make her feel better, so I'd give her a hug and that seemed to work, because she stopped crying.

Then I knew for sure that my parents were not friends anymore, because my Dad packed his suitcase and moved away. He now lives by himself in a house in town. When Dad left, he gave me a big hug. He told me that he loved me and that he would see me soon.

After this happened, I felt sad. Sometimes I thought it was my fault. Maybe if I listened more or did better at school, my parents would be friends again? My Mum and Dad kept telling me it was not my fault that they forgot how to be friends. I believed them, but . . . sometimes I still wondered if it really was my fault.

Mum and Dad explained to me that sometimes parents get along better when they live in different houses. They said that no matter where they lived, they would both always love me and be there for me.

They were right! After my Dad moved to a different house, things started to change.

My Mum and Dad didn't look as sad as they did before.
This made me feel better and much happier.

Even though I live at home with my Mum, I phone my Dad as often as I want and visit him every week. Sometimes I stay overnight at Dad's house, and it's so much fun. We like to play games or read together. The best part is that we laugh a lot.

On special days, like my birthday, Dad comes over to my house so we can have a family night together. It's just like old times! We play board games or watch a movie. We even laugh together. My Mum and Dad may not live in the same house, but we are still a family, and our time together seems extra special.

Now I can see that even though my parents forgot how to be friends, it doesn't mean they don't love me or that they stop being my parents. The time I spend with each of my parents is special. We're not all together, but we all seem happier. The arguing has finally stopped.

My Mum and Dad will always love me and are always bugging me to do my homework. They take turns picking me up from school, and whenever I have a basketball game, they are both there to cheer me on! I love my Mum and my Dad. They are the best!

Note to Parents

Growing up in a one-parent family was certainly tough! As a child I did not understand the dynamics of the situation or the struggles which led to my parents' decision to live apart. Initially, I blamed myself for my parents' behaviour. I would spend countless hours trying to figure out what 'I' had done to contribute to my family's difficulties.

I still remember the day when my Mum sat me down and took the time to explain to me what had happened in our family. That was the day that many of my fears and anxieties were alleviated. Not only did I learn what to expect of my parents and of the situation as a whole, but most importantly I learned that my parents' decision to live apart was not my fault.

Given my personal experience as well as my work with families in my role as a social worker, I recognise and appreciate a child's need to seek understanding in regard to his/her family's situation. Every child has the right to be heard and to have his/her feelings respected.

The purpose of *When my parents forgot how to be friends* is to acknowledge some of the concerns and anxieties your child may experience during this change within your family unit. Allowing your child the opportunity to explore his/her feelings and fears is the first step in the process of healing. Giving your child the chance to heal, by addressing some of these issues, will encourage him/her to become a survivor of separation and divorce, rather than remaining a victim.

This book can also be used as a tool to initiate dialogue and to stimulate communication between you and your children. Your children will be reminded that they are not responsible for the difficulties within the family and that their behaviour had no impact on your decision to separate.

Taking the time to read to your child is a wonderful way to share a moment together. Children are important, and what they think and how they feel matters. Let's do our part to show our children that we truly care!

Other titles in this series:
My friend has Down's syndrome
I remember
Lost and found
Have you got a secret?
Daddy's getting married
Colours of the rainbow
My brother is autistic

Published in Great Britain in MMXIII by
Book House, an imprint of
The Salariya Book Company Ltd
25 Marlborough Place, Brighton BN1 1UB
www.salariya.com
www.book-house.co.uk

1 3 5 7 9 8 6 4 2

A CIP catalogue record for this book is available
from the British Library.

Printed and bound in China.

PB ISBN: 978-1-908973-23-8

Visit our **new** online shop at
shop.salariya.com
for great offers, gift ideas, all our new
releases and free postage and packaging.

Original title of the book in Spanish:
Cuando Mis Padres se Olvidaron de Ser Amigos
© Copyright MMV by Gemser Publications, S.L.
El Castell, 38; Teià (08329) Barcelona, Spain (World Rights)